FORENSIC SCIENCE INVESTIGATED

FORENSIC|TECHNIQUES

WRITTEN BY:
Rebecca Stefoff

Marshall Cavendish
Benchmark
New York

MARSHALL CAVENDISH BENCHMARK
99 WHITE PLAINS ROAD
TARRYTOWN, NEW YORK 10591-5502
www.marshallcavendish.us

LIBRARY OF CONGRESS CATALOGING-IN-PUBLICATION DATA
Stefoff, Rebecca, 1951-
Forensic techniques / by Rebecca Stefoff.
p. cm. — (Forensic science investigated)
Includes bibliographical references and index.
ISBN 978-0-7614-3083-4
1. Forensic sciences—Juvenile literature. I. Title.
HV8073.S732 2009
363.25—dc22
2008003638

EDITOR: Christina Gardeski   PUBLISHER: Michelle Bisson
ART DIRECTOR: Anahid Hamparian   SERIES DESIGNER: Kristen Branch

Photo Research by Anne Burns Images

Front Cover Photo by *Phototake*/Terry Why   Back Cover Photo by *Phototake*/Terry Why

The photographs in this book are used with permission and through the courtesy of:
iStockphoto: pp. 1, 3 (hand Chris Hutchinson, cells David Marchal). *Phototake*: p. 4 Terry
Why. *Corbis*: p. 7 Marco Cristofori; p. 14 Marc Serota/Reuters; p. 30 Holger
Winkler/A.B./zefa; p. 64 Galen Rowell; p. 83 Corbis. *Art Resource*: p. 8 Nimatallah. *The
Image Works*: p. 10 Albert Harlingue/Roger Viollet; p. 28 Roger Viollet. *Photo Researchers*:
p. 21 Michael Donne; pp. 37, 60, 63 Mauro Fermariello; p. 40 Alfred Pasieka; p. 44 Tek
Image; p. 45 Jim Varney; p. 47 James King-Holmes. *Alamy Images*: p. 24 A.T. Willet;
pp. 53, 58 Mikael Karlsson; p. 55 Vario Images GmbH & Co. KG; p. 78 Ian
Miles/Flashpoint Pictures. *Associated Press*: pp. 26, 35, 50. *Mammoth Lakes Police
Department*: pp. 67, 68, 69, 76.

Printed in Malaysia
1 3 5 6 4 2

Cover: Fingerprinting is a key part of modern forensic science.

CONTENTS

Dental records, facial reconstruction, and the careful examination of crime scene evidence are just a few of the tools of forensics, which is the use of science to solve crimes.

WHAT IS
FORENSICS?

AN OLD MAN DIES WHEN his house burns down. It looks like a tragic accident—until investigators find traces of an accelerant, a substance used to start fires or to make them burn hotter and faster. Police then discover that the old man's nephew, who would have gotten the money from his uncle's life insurance policy, recently bought a large container of the accelerant.

A hit-and-run driver strikes a boy on a bicycle. The car leaves a few tiny flakes of paint on the boy's clothes and on the mangled frame of his bike. The bits of paint are almost invisible to the unaided eye, but they are big enough to lead police to the car and the guilty driver.

"My wife just shot herself!" a man cries out to the operator at the emergency 911 number. Deputies from the sheriff's office find the dead woman slumped in a chair with a shotgun in her hands. They make a detailed photographic record of the scene. A crime scene specialist reviews the photographs and reports that the evidence does not match the husband's story. According to the size and shape of the blood spatters on the wall behind the chair, the woman was shot from ten feet away, while she was standing up. Why would the husband lie? There is only one reason. He murdered his wife—but drops of her blood had pointed to the truth.

Each of these cases was solved with the help of **forensic science**, which is the use of scientific methods and tools to investigate crimes and bring suspects to trial. The term "forensic" comes from ancient Rome, where people debated matters of law in a public meeting place called the Forum. The Latin word *forum* gave rise to *forensic*, meaning "relating to courts of law or to public debate." Today the term "**forensics**" has several meanings. One is the art of speaking in debates, which is why some schools have forensics clubs or teams for students who want to learn debating skills. The best-known meaning of "forensics," though, is crime solving through forensic science.

▲ Visitors explore the remains of Rome's ancient Forum, the meeting place that gave forensics its name.

Fascination with forensics explains the popularity of many recent TV shows, movies, and books, but crime and science have been linked for a long time. The first science used in criminal investigation was medicine, and one of the earliest reports of forensic medicine is more than two thousand years old. In 44 BCE, the Roman leader Julius Caesar was stabbed to death not far from the Forum. A physician named Antistius examined the body and found that Caesar had

▲ Julius Caesar was reportedly assassinated by a group of men. Although a physician pinpointed the stab wound that killed Caesar, he could not name the killer.

received twenty-three stab wounds, but only one wound was fatal.

Antistius had performed one of history's first recorded **postmortem** examinations, in which a physician looks at a body to find out how the person died. But forensics has always had limits. Antistius could point out the chest wound that had killed Caesar, but he could not say who had struck the deadly blow.

Death in its many forms inspired the first forensic manuals. The oldest one was published in China in 1248. Called *Hsi duan yu* (The Washing Away of Wrongs), it tells how the bodies of people who have been strangled differ from those of drowning victims. When a corpse is recovered from the water, says the manual, officers of the law should examine the tissues and small bones in the neck. Torn tissues and broken bones show that the victim met with foul play before being thrown into the water.

Poison became another landmark in the history of forensics in 1813, when Mathieu Orfila, a professor of medical and forensic chemistry at the University of Paris, published *Traité des poisons* (Treatise on Poisons). Orfila described the deadly effects of various mineral, vegetable, and animal substances. He laid the foundation of the modern science of **toxicology**, the branch of forensics that deals with poisons and drugs, and their effects on the human body.

As France's most famous expert on poisons, Orfila played a part in an 1840 criminal trial that received wide publicity. Marie LaFarge was accused of murder after her husband died. Orfila testified that he had examined the husband's corpse and found traces of arsenic. LaFarge insisted that she had not fed the arsenic to her husband and that he must have eaten it while away

▲ In a sensational 1840 trial, Marie LaFarge was convicted of poisoning her husband. The trial established toxicology, the study of foreign substances in the body, as part of criminal investigation.

from home. The court, however, sentenced her to life imprisonment. Pardoned in 1850 after ten years in prison, LaFarge died the next year, claiming innocence to the end.

Cases such as the LaFarge trial highlighted the growing use of medical evidence in criminal investigations and trials. Courts were recognizing other kinds of forensic evidence, too. As early as 1784, a British murder case had been decided by physical evidence. The torn edge of a piece of newspaper found in the pocket of a suspect named John Toms matched the torn edge of a ball of paper found in the wound of a man who had been killed by a pistol shot to the head (at the time, people used rolled pieces of cloth or paper, called wadding, to hold bullets firmly in gun barrels). Because the paper was a clear link to the deadly shot, Toms was declared guilty of murder. In 1835, an officer of Scotland Yard, Britain's famous police division, caught a murderer by using a flaw on the fatal bullet to trace the bullet to its maker. Such cases marked the birth of **ballistics**, the branch of forensics that deals with firearms.

Not all forensic developments involved murder. Science also helped solve crimes such as arson and forgery. By the early nineteenth century, chemists had developed the first tests to identify certain dyes used in ink. Experts could then determine the age and chemical makeup of the ink on documents, such as wills and valuable manuscripts, that were suspected of being fakes.

Forensics started to become a regular part of police work at the end of the nineteenth century, after an Austrian law professor named Hans Gross published a two-volume handbook on the subject in 1893. Gross's book, usually referred to as *Criminal Investigation*, brought together all the many techniques that scientists and law enforcers had developed for examining the physical evidence of crime—bloodstains, bullets, and more. Police departments started using *Criminal Investigation* to train officers. The book entered law school courses as well.

Modern forensics experts regard Hans Gross as the founder of their profession. Among other contributions, Gross invented the word "**criminalistics**." He used it to refer to the general study of crime or criminals. Today, however, criminalistics has a narrower, more specific meaning. It refers to the study of physical evidence from crime scenes.

Almost every branch of science has been involved in criminal investigations. Meteorologists have testified about the weather on the date of a crime. Botanists have named the plants that produced tiny specks of pollen found on suspects' clothes. Dentists have matched bite marks on victims' bodies to the teeth of their killers. Criminalistics—the collecting, protecting, and examining of crime scene evidence—is the basis for these and other forms of forensic investigation. Whether they are called criminalists, crime scene investigators (CSIs), or scene-of-crime officers (SOCOs), the men and women who work with the physical and biological signs of crime are the first to give the evidence a chance to speak—to reveal what really happened.

After a driver reported seeing a gunman near this Florida middle school, police closed and searched the potential crime scene. No gunman was found. The call may have been a hoax, but law enforcement must take such calls seriously.

CHAPTER ONE

THE SCENE OF THE CRIME

▼ YOU'VE SEEN IT ON TELEVISION,

in movies, maybe in real life. Sirens blare and lights flash as police cars fill the street. A fire truck and an ambulance pull up. Uniformed police officers cordon off a section of sidewalk or an entire building with bright yellow plastic tape marked "Do Not Cross."

A crowd of curious onlookers grows larger by the second, and cops patrol the tape to keep people from sneaking into the protected zone—or out of it. Then the TV news vans arrive. Reporters and camera operators pile out and start interviewing bystanders. A buzz of questions and comments fills the air.

A crime scene can look like pure chaos from the outside. Inside the taped-off area, though, activity usually follows a well-organized plan. Police and others who answer emergency calls understand the importance of a crime scene. The physical evidence there is vital to investigating the crime and, if all goes well, bringing a suspect to trial.

▶ PROCESSING THE SCENE

One of the most important jobs in forensics is processing crime scenes. Processing a scene means surveying it, recording it in detail, examining it for evidence, and collecting the evidence. Each of these tasks must be carried out in the right way, because mistakes or shortcomings in crime scene processing can destroy vital evidence or weaken the case when it comes to court. Something as simple as a crime scene investigator failing to write down whether a door was locked or unlocked could eventually result in a case being dismissed and a suspect who may have been guilty going free.

Still, not all crime scenes are created equal. Law enforcement resources are limited by such things as the size of the local police or sheriff's department, the equipment and staff of the local or regional crime lab, and the backlog of evidence waiting to be analyzed.

Because authorities cannot perform a full forensic examination of every crime, they must devote their resources to the more serious cases. If a parked car is stolen from the street, for example, the police probably will not dust the neighboring cars for fingerprints. But in the case of a carjacking, when someone attacks a driver and then steals the car, investigators will gather all possible evidence and information from the victim, because the crime involved violence against a person. A large crime scene or mass disaster, such as a school shooting or airplane crash, may call upon forensic experts from a wide area, reducing the resources that are immediately available for less spectacular incidents.

▶ FIRST THINGS FIRST

When police—or fire or ambulance crews—are first to arrive at a crime scene, they have certain responsibilities. Although each responsibility is important, some are more urgent than others. Crime scene procedures are usually based on a list of priorities like this one:

1. *Saving lives.* The first task of a law enforcement, medical, or firefighting professional who arrives at a crime scene is to save lives and help anyone who is injured or in danger. Search-and-rescue operations, first aid, and escorting people out of danger are top priorities. The first responders are also responsible for making sure that the scene is safe for emergency medical

technicians (EMTs), crime scene investigators, and others who come later.

2. *Detaining suspects.* Next in importance to saving lives is holding suspects. Depending on the circumstances, law enforcement officers may arrest people who are known or suspected of being involved in the crime, or hold them for questioning. Suspects are usually asked to provide identification, and they are searched. Suspects must also be removed from the crime scene as soon as possible, to keep them from tampering with evidence.

3. *Securing the scene.* Once suspects are under control, the next task is to secure the crime scene. Securing a scene means controlling it to keep the public from moving in and out of it. If the crime scene is a house, for example, securing it can mean stationing an officer at each corner to make sure nothing passes through a door or window. Police usually use crime scene tape to seal off driveways and sidewalks leading to houses. They also use it to set up a barrier around any outdoor scene. If evidence is in danger of being destroyed, such as by fire or weather, the first

arrivals on the scene may have to collect material in a hurry instead of in the careful, methodical way preferred by forensic experts. Otherwise, the task of examining the scene usually falls to forensic specialists.

4. *Identifying witnesses.* Anyone who witnessed the crime—or who saw something possibly connected with the crime, such as a car speeding away after a gunshot—may have information useful to investigators. Law enforcement officials will get the names and addresses of all potential witnesses and will take witnesses' statements. It is important to keep the witnesses from talking among themselves, if possible. Their testimony is more likely to be accurate, and is more valuable in court, if it is based only on what they remember seeing, not on conversations with others at the scene.

▶ RECORDING AND SEARCHING THE SCENE

When the urgent business of saving lives and controlling suspects is out of the way, it is time to examine the crime scene. Depending on the size and type of the crime, and also on the staff and resources available, this task may be carried out by some or all of the following people:

- police officers or sheriff's deputies (who may have received some training in handling evidence)
- evidence technicians (who usually have been trained to collect evidence in the field but may not be qualified to analyze it)
- criminalists or crime scene investigators (who usually hold degrees or certifications in forensics; many criminalists have multiple duties at crime scenes, but larger law enforcement departments have teams of criminalists with various specialties, such as photography or fingerprinting)
- forensic scientists (who work in law enforcement departments, universities, or private companies; scientists typically do not do fieldwork, but the officer in charge of an unusually challenging case may call experts to the crime scene)

▶ DOCUMENTING THE SCENE

One responsibility of crime scene investigators is to make an accurate record of the scene when it is as close to its original state as possible. Documentation can include notes, sketches, photographs, and videos.

Notes are usually the first records of a crime scene. The officers who answer a call should record as many details as possible, as soon as possible. In addition to listing the witnesses, they should describe the condition

▲ A scene-of-crime officer (SOCO) photographs a gun found at a crime scene. The yellow evidence marker will show the gun's location in crime scene photographs. To keep from contaminating the scene, the SOCO wears disposable gloves, shoe covers, cap, mask, and suit.

of the crime scene. Were doors open or closed? Did the officers notice any smells or sounds at the scene? Did anyone report something unusual in the area? The first arrivals on the crime scene should also keep a log of everyone who arrives, including ambulance drivers, news reporters, relatives and friends of the victim, and other law enforcement people.

When the forensic examination of the scene is under way, an evidence technician or criminalist takes over, making detailed notes about how the scene looks and where each piece of evidence is located. These notes may be made in writing or spoken into a tape recorder. The criminalist may also sketch the crime scene. After a murder in a park, for example, a sketch would include an outline of the body, with a compass arrow showing the direction in which the body lay. Nearby features such as trees, benches, and paths would be labeled, with arrows showing the distance between each object and the body.

Photography is essential to documenting crime scenes. A photo can capture evidence that would otherwise be lost, such as a trail of wet footprints or a bruise. Making photographs that are useful to investigators and later will stand up to scrutiny in court, however, requires special techniques. Although many general criminalists are good photographers, forensic photographers specialize in producing high-quality images of crime scenes and evidence.

Photographing a crime scene is done in three stages. First, the photographer takes establishing shots. These pictures show the overall crime scene and its relationship to the setting. For that murder in the park, the establishing shots would show the entrance to the park, the route to the victim's body, and the landscape around the body.

Next the photographer takes mid-range shots. These show specific features of the scene—the body, a bloody fingerprint on a park bench, a broken branch on a bush that might be a sign of struggle. The photographer will probably place rulers or specially marked forensic measuring scales next to the evidence. Later, people looking at the photos will be able to use these reference points to judge the size of the objects photographed and their relationship to one another.

Finally the photographer takes detail photos, close-up pictures of individual pieces of evidence, such as bite marks, crumpled pieces of paper, and fingerprints. Again, scales are included in the photographs to show the size and orientation of each item.

Many crime scene photographers use both digital and film cameras. Digital cameras let photographers see

▲ This footprint left at a crime scene was made by a size-nine Phat Farm shoe. To match a print, criminalists may turn to collections of shoe-print images.

results at once, so they can be sure that they took the picture they wanted. Digital cameras, however, are not yet as good as film cameras at taking high-contrast, black-and-white images, the kind preferred for fingerprints, for example. In addition, digital photographs have less value than film photos as evidence, because most people know that digital images are easier to alter or tamper with than photos on film. As a result, the forensic photographer's standby is still a high-quality film camera with an assortment of lenses and film types.

Video cameras are also used at many crime scenes. Although video does not work well for documenting details of evidence, it can capture establishing images of the general setting, which can be helpful to both criminalists and jurors. Video cameras are also useful for creating a visual record of arrivals, departures, and what was said and done during the examination of the crime scene.

▶ SEARCHING THE SCENE

Sometimes a crime scene photographer searches the scene, looking for evidence to record. At other times the photographer gets instructions from the criminalists who are searching the site. Various search patterns exist, so investigators must choose the pattern that best suits the scene and the resources.

A lane search is ideal for a large outdoor crime scene, for example, but it requires many searchers. They line up side by side, facing in the same direction, and then move forward slowly, each examining a lane that may be only a yard (meter) wide. For a single searcher, on the other hand, a spiral pattern is a good choice. The searcher moves outward in larger and larger circles from the center of the crime scene, or inward in smaller and smaller circles from its edge. Other patterns divide the area into zones or a grid of crossing

▲ Investigators search an outdoor crime scene in Lakewood, Washington, looking for evidence that might help identify the killer of a ten-year-old girl.

lanes. In each case, the idea is to search systematically, not randomly, so that nothing is overlooked.

Ideally, the searchers and everyone else at a crime scene will wear protective gear, including hair covers, gloves, shoe covers, and disposable sterile suits that are worn over their clothing. The gear prevents evidence exchange—something that can both help and hurt a criminal investigation.

Evidence exchange (also called evidence transfer) can be summed up as "every contact leaves a trace," meaning that every time two objects or people come into contact, they leave physical traces on each other. Workers at a crime scene must take care not to contaminate the scene by shedding hair or leaving behind dirt from their shoes or fibers from their clothing. None of the evidence gathered at the scene should come from the investigators themselves, because that could get in the way of identifying traces left by the criminal.

Yet evidence transfer can be a criminalist's best friend. Evidence transfer means that a criminal always leaves some evidence, however tiny and hard to find, at the crime scene. At the same time, the crime or crime scene leaves evidence on the criminal. The crime may be solved from either end. If a hit-and-run driver strikes a bicyclist, for example, the breakthrough may come when someone spots blood or fibers from the cyclist's clothes on the crumpled bumper of a suspect's car, or when a forensic technician analyzes paint that the car deposited on the victim's clothing.

The final stage in crime scene processing is collecting and removing the evidence. Some of it will go to crime labs for analysis. Some will be stored until the case comes to trial. And in cases that involve death, the first and most important piece of evidence will go to the office of the **medical examiner (ME)**, the public official responsible for examining bodies.

LOCARD'S EXCHANGE PRINCIPLE

"EVERY CONTACT LEAVES A TRACE" is an idea first stated by Edmond Locard, a leading French forensic scientist of the early twentieth century. In a 1923 manual for police officers, Locard wrote, "It is impossible for a criminal to act . . . without leaving traces of his presence."

Above: After studying both medicine and law, Edmond Locard devoted his energies to forensic science. He remained active in investigation and research until his death in 1966 at the age of 89.

· · · · ·

This idea is often called the evidence exchange principle, or Locard's Exchange Principle, although Locard never used that phrase.

Locard knew the power of trace evidence. In 1912 he had proved that a man named Emile Gourbin had strangled his lover by showing that bits of matter scraped from beneath Gourbin's fingernails were flecks of skin and pinkish face powder that matched those of the dead woman. Criminalists still use the same technique of scraping and analyzing material from under the nails of suspects and victims. In other ways, though, the study of trace evidence has changed dramatically since Locard's time. In his day, for example, a determined criminal could wash away bloodstains. Today's investigators use a variety of tools, including special light sources and chemical sprays that glow upon contact with blood, to locate even a tiny, diluted droplet that would be invisible to the unaided eye.

· · · · ·

One important piece of evidence has already been removed from this crime scene. The victim's body, now represented by a chalk outline, has been taken to a medical examiner, who will officially determine the cause of death.

CHAPTER TWO

THE MANNER OF DEATH

▼ EVERY DEATH IS EITHER NATURAL,

an accident, a suicide, or a homicide. Most deaths are due to natural causes. But when someone dies by violence, or suddenly and unexpectedly, or without having been under a doctor's care, it is up to the medical examiner to determine the cause of death.

▶ TECHNIQUES OF FORENSIC PATHOLOGY

Determining the manner and specific cause of death is called forensic pathology. It is both a medical and a legal process. Forensic pathologists in the medical examiner's office follow a series of steps when they investigate a death.

The first step is to examine the body at the crime scene. The general circumstances may hold clues to the cause of death—but these clues can be misleading. A body fished out of a river, for example, is not necessarily a drowning victim. He or she might have had a fatal heart attack, or received a deadly blow to the head, before falling into the water.

Bodies are often moved by family members, bystanders, or emergency medical workers before forensic teams arrive. Even when the crime scene has been disturbed in this way, the pathologist can learn something by examining the body at the scene, before it is moved again. The temperature, color, and stiffness of the body help the pathologist determine the time of death, especially during the first 48 hours or so. The pathologist also checks for any obvious signs of trauma, or injury. After the body has been photographed and examined in place, police officers or forensic technicians take it to a medical laboratory called a morgue. The morgue can be either attached to a crime lab or located in a hospital.

At the morgue, the dead person is the subject of a general survey called the postmortem, or after-death, examination. In addition to a forensic pathologist and an assistant, the postmortem team may include an evidence technician, a police officer, and a photographer to document it all. The victim's clothes are checked for evidence, which is bagged and labeled, and then the clothing is removed and turned over to the evidence specialists. The pathologist takes scrapings from under the fingernails, draws blood samples (if this was not done at the crime scene), and clips a strand of the victim's hair for comparison with other evidence.

The postmortem team then scans the body for signs of violence. Experienced criminalists can tell a lot by looking at wounds. Certain injuries, such as cuts across the palms of the hands or broken fingers, are defensive wounds. They show that the victim tried to protect himself or herself from a killer who was close at hand, probably wielding a knife or club. The shape and angle of stab wounds tell investigators something about the weapon that was used, and also about the relative positions of the killer and the victim. Other signs of trauma may be harder to find. A needle used to administer poison, for example, leaves only a tiny mark.

Distinctive features of the body, such as tattoos or birthmarks, are noted during the postmortem. These are especially important in cases where a victim's name is unknown, because they may lead to an identification. After the initial examination, the body is washed, scanned, and photographed again. For purposes of identification, fingerprints may be taken at this point. If identification remains in doubt, a forensic anthropologist may later be called in to examine the remains. Anthropology is the study of similarities and differences among various human groups, and forensic anthropologists use clues such as bone length and skull shape to make educated guesses about the gender, age, and ethnic background of a victim. Even if all that remains of a victim are a few bones, a forensic anthropologist may offer insights vital to the investigation.

The final phase of the postmortem is an **autopsy**. In this procedure, the pathologist dissects the body to pinpoint the cause of death. Wielding a grisly-sounding set of tools, including scalpels, bone cutters, skull saws, and brain knives, the pathologist starts by investigating obvious wounds or injuries. A long cut up from below the navel to the neck, then another one across from shoulder to shoulder, lets the pathologist open the torso and remove the organs. Each organ is weighed and preserved for further study. (At this point the pathologist will find out whether that body recovered from the river has water in the lungs. If not, the victim did not drown.)

The pathologist may also open the skull to remove the brain, which can be analyzed for signs of a stroke or other potentially fatal medical condition as well as

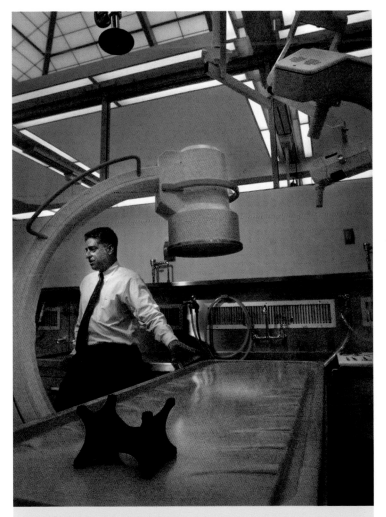

▲ At a state-of-the-art forensic laboratory in Nashville, Tennessee, the main autopsy room has four of these stations, each equipped with tools for examining and photographing the bodies of crime victims.

for signs of injury. If the pathologist decides that the organs and brain should be examined in detail, a histologist, a specialist in analyzing tissues under the microscope, is called in.

The postmortem and autopsy cannot always pinpoint the manner or the exact cause of death. Death by drowning, for example, can be accident, suicide, or murder—but unless the body has bruises shaped suspiciously like handprints, proving that the victim was pushed off a bridge may be impossible. The pathologist's ability to recover information may also be severely limited when the body is badly decomposed or missing some parts. Still, forensic pathology can often establish a victim's cause of death beyond doubt, or at least rule out certain possibilities.

▶ BLOOD STUDIES

Investigators can learn a lot about a crime from blood—if they find it and identify it. The first step is physical examination of blood evidence, which is usually performed by a criminalist. Physical examination starts with locating blood traces at crime scenes, often by using chemical sprays to highlight blood that may not be readily visible, such as dried fragments of blood between floorboards or tiles. Traces of blood can linger in cracks even after a killer has vigorously mopped the

▲ A lab technician adds antibodies for blood group B to a series of blood samples. The antibodies will react with any samples that belong to blood group B.

floor. Another kind of physical blood examination is studying the pattern of spill or spatter. The shape of a blood droplet tells the criminalist the direction and speed at which the droplet was traveling when it hit a floor, a wall, or other surface. This, in turn, can reveal details about the injury that caused the bleeding.

The next step is forensic serology, which is the medical analysis of blood—or evidence that might be blood—for a criminal investigation. Using a series of tests, serologists determine whether a substance really is blood. Next, they find out whether it is animal or human blood. This is done by exposing a sample of the blood to a substance called an antiserum, which is formed when blood from one species is injected into a creature of another species. If a rabbit receives blood from a human, for example, the rabbit's blood will produce an antiserum to human blood. That antiserum can then be isolated from the rabbit's blood and used in serological testing.

When a serologist applies human antiserum to a sample of human blood, a chemical reaction causes crystals of solid material to form in the sample. But if human antiserum is applied to blood that is *not* human, nothing happens. Crime labs are typically stocked with a variety of prepared antiserums so that forensic serologists can test not just for human blood but also for common animal species—such as dogs, cats, and livestock—that may have left blood at a crime scene.

Once blood has been identified as human, the serologist wants to know whose blood it is. If the investigators think that the blood belongs to a known victim, suspect, or bystander, they can compare the evidence directly to a sample from that person. (A sample from a known source is called an exemplar.) The most thorough way to compare evidence and exemplar is to analyze DNA from both, but DNA tests can be costly. Serologists usually start with a faster, simpler test that determines the blood type, or group, of the evidence and the exemplar. All human blood belongs to one of four types: A, B, AB, or O. If the evidence and exemplar are different types, they are from different people. If they are the same type, they *may* be from the same person. To find out, the serologist will use DNA analysis.

DNA analysis is a complex and sometimes controversial process that many members of the public, including jurors, do not understand. One reason for confusion is that DNA tests are constantly changing as new techniques are developed. Today several kinds of DNA can be used for forensic purposes, depending on the amount of sample material available and the questions investigators hope to answer.

"A genetic fingerprint" is how many people think of DNA, and there is some truth in the phrase. DNA is deoxyribonucleic acid, which exists in long, spiral-shaped strands called chromosomes in the nucleus, or center, of living cells. DNA can be found in cells from all parts of the human body, including blood, saliva, bone marrow, tissue, skin, hair, and other bodily fluids. Because the amount of DNA obtained from samples is generally very small, forensic serologists use a chemical process called the

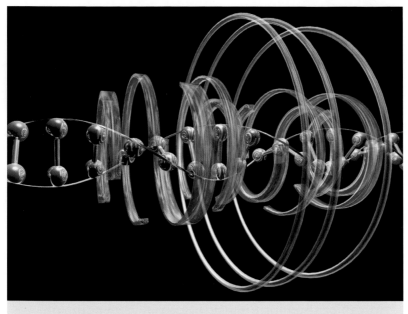

▲ Computer-generated artwork shows a strand of DNA (the pink strands linked by rods) producing messenger RNA (the blue bands) that will create proteins, the building blocks of cells.

polymerase chain reaction (PCR) to copy the DNA millions of times. This increases the amount of DNA available for testing.

Sections of the chromosomes called genes contain the codes for the inherited traits that shape living organisms. Each species, or variety, of living thing has a unique set of genetic material called its genome. Within a genome, however, an enormous number of individual variations are possible. How enormous? To test human DNA, forensic serologists use a standard profile based on thirteen loci, or points, on the long DNA molecule. Some researchers have estimated that the odds of two people sharing the same thirteen-locus DNA profile are 200 billion to one. Others say the odds are even smaller: one in a trillion. Either way, it is extremely unlikely that two people will have DNA that matches at the same thirteen points.

Unlikely—but not entirely impossible. **DNA testing** cannot guarantee that two samples are from the same person. It can only give the statistical likelihood that they are a match. The reliability of the match drops if the samples are incomplete, very old, or contaminated.

Law enforcement agencies around the world are building up databases of DNA profiles in the same way that they have created databases of fingerprints. One such database, created by the FBI, is the Combined DNA Index System (CODIS), which holds millions of DNA profiles of convicted criminals. Investigators starting a new case can compare any DNA found at the scene with the samples stored in the database. This may link the sample to someone whose identity is known.

Other countries' law enforcement agencies are developing similar databases, although countries have different standards about whose DNA can be included. Some anticrime activists want everyone's DNA to be recorded in a database that would eventually include the entire population. Other people see this idea as an alarming violation of civil rights and privacy, saying that DNA databases should be limited to criminals. Yet DNA testing has grown into a vitally important part of modern crime detection, and the number of labs that can perform the tests is increasing. With DNA evidence recognized as an outstandingly clear connection between a suspect and a crime scene or victim, DNA databases will undoubtedly play an ever-growing role in law enforcement.

DNA matching may connect a suspect to a crime scene, but by itself, without any other evidence, it may not be enough to prove that the suspect committed the crime. DNA analysis is a very useful technique, however, for exclusion, which means ruling *out* suspects. In recent years, people imprisoned for crimes such as murder and rape have been freed after new DNA tests on the biological evidence used to convict them proved that the evidence had come from someone else.

▶ TOXICOLOGY

Poison is an ancient weapon. It has been used by many writers of murder mysteries as well as killers. Today, however, crimes using traditional poisons such as arsenic, strychnine, and cyanide are uncommon.

Poisoning is more likely to occur as the result of a drug overdose or through the misuse of ordinary products, such as drain cleaner and bug spray, that contain harmful substances. Carbon monoxide, an odorless, colorless gas, kills people every year by accident or suicide. People are also accidentally poisoned by eating deadly mushrooms and by the stings or bites of venomous animals, such as coral snakes and brown recluse spiders.

Poisonous or harmful substances are called toxins. The study of toxins in crime solving is forensic toxicology, a branch of forensics that is now more often concerned with drugs and environmental hazards than with homicide by poison.

One of a forensic toxicologist's main activities is testing to see whether toxins are present in biological samples from crime suspects and victims. A sample could be a breath from a driver suspected of being drunk; a strand of hair from someone suspected of using cocaine or another illegal drug; urine from an athlete accused of taking steroids or other banned performance enhancers; or blood and tissue from an elderly person who died mysteriously in a nursing home.

In addition to testing biological samples for chemicals, forensic toxicologists spend a lot of time analyzing materials, usually checking to see whether suspicious

▲ A motorist suspected of driving under the influence of alcohol
   blows into an instrument called a breathalyzer. It will tell if his
   bloodstream contains more than the legal limit of alcohol.

materials are illegal drugs. A toxicologist can do more
than tell whether a packet of white powder is heroin. By
analyzing the chemical makeup of the sample for traces
of contaminants, a toxicologist may be able to tell
whether the material came from the same illegal drug
lab as another sample. Such clues are valuable to agents
who are trying to track down the source of drugs.

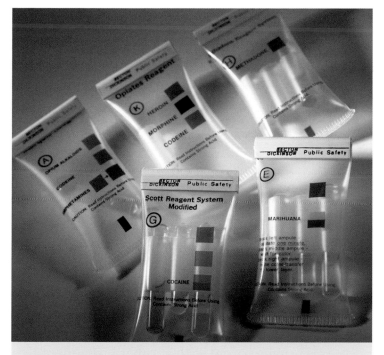

▲ Using these drug kits, investigators can test samples of material to see whether they are illegal drugs, such as heroin, cocaine, or marijuana.

There are two general kinds of toxicological test, presumptive and confirmatory. Toxicologists usually start with presumptive tests, which can identify the general category of drug or poison. For these tests, the toxicologist applies substances that are known to produce chemical reactions—usually color changes—when they come in contact with certain types of toxins.

Once a presumptive test has shown that the sample contains a drug or poison, the toxicologist moves on to more complicated procedures called confirmatory tests, which are designed to identify and measure specific toxins.

Some toxicological tests, such as breath analysis or infrared breath testing, are simple enough to be performed on the spot by traffic officers who are checking to see whether a driver has consumed too much alcohol. Other toxicological tests require sophisticated instruments that are used in a crime lab.

One of a forensic toxicologist's most important pieces of equipment is the gas chromatograph (GC), which turns a sample of the test material into a vapor and separates the resulting gas into its component parts. It is usually paired with another instrument that measures the rate at which different chemicals in the vapor move through a column of liquid or of solid particles. This type of instrumentation is used in a presumptive test to narrow the field of possible toxins by identifying the general kinds of chemicals that are present in the sample.

After the presumptive step, the examiner performs a confirmatory test to pinpoint the specific chemical or chemicals found during the screening. (A forensic chemist might go directly to confirmatory testing in a

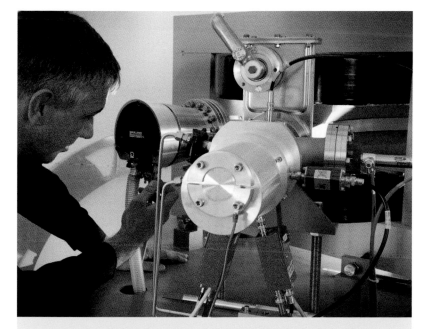

▲ An accelerator mass spectrometer (AMS) measures the amount of different kinds of carbon in tissue samples from organic material, such as bone, flesh, or wood. The results tell how long ago the source of the tissue sample died. This test, called carbon dating, is an archaeologist's tool that is also used in medical and forensic research.

case where there is other evidence, such as a witness's testimony, about what substances could be present in the sample.) Forensic chemists often perform confirmatory tests by passing a sample directly from the gas chromatograph to another instrument called a mass spectrometer, in a combination known as a GC-MS.

The mass spectrometer further analyzes the vapor, allowing the toxicologist to identify each specific ingredient the sample contains, as well as the quantity of the various ingredients. This level of detail can pinpoint the distinctive features of individual batches of drugs.

Pathologists, serologists, and toxicologists study bodies, blood, and toxins. Their branches of forensic science have much in common with the practice of medicine. Criminalists, however, work with many other kinds of evidence. Using a wide range of techniques, they unravel the meaning of clues as varied as fingerprints, bullets, and stray carpet fibers and cat hairs.

DOWN ON THE BODY FARM

NOT FAR FROM Knoxville, Tennessee, is a three-acre piece of land planted with corpses. The place is often called the Body Farm, although its real name is the University of Tennessee Forensic Anthropology Facility. Since 1971 it has given forensic scientists a rare chance to study taphonomy, the physical changes in a body after death.

Hundreds of bodies have decayed, decomposed, or dried up on the Body Farm. Many of them were unclaimed corpses from medical examiners' labs. Others were donated by people who wanted their remains to advance forensic science. The corpses have been sunk in ponds, left unburied on the ground, buried at different depths in varying kinds of soil, even tied to trees. Researchers have learned a lot by recording how each body changes over time.

Work at the Body Farm has helped with one of the most challenging tasks in forensics: determining the time of death. Measurements of maggot and insect activity in the corpses have given investigators a powerful new tool for estimating the death interval, or time since death, in bodies that have been dead for more than a few days. In addition, the facility lets investigators—from FBI agents to search dogs—practice hunting for buried and hidden bodies. Plans are under way for similar research facilities in other climates, and much remains to be learned about the human body after death. Forensic anthropologist William Bass, founder of the Body Farm, said in 2004, "I think we've just scratched the surface."

A forensic scientist removes potential evidence, such as hairs and loose threads, from a suspect's jeans. A tiny piece of evidence may be enough to link the suspect to the crime scene or the victim.

CHAPTER THREE

THE TALE OF THE
EVIDENCE

▼ HISTORIANS OF CRIME THINK THAT

the first person ever found guilty of murder because of fingerprints was a woman in Argentina, who was convicted in 1892. Before that time, a few writers had noted that fingerprints seemed to be highly individual. Some people thought that fingerprints might be a handy form of identification, because people who did not know how to write could use them as a substitute for a signature. Henry Faulds, a Scottish doctor living in Japan, had even suggested in 1880 that fingerprints left at crime scenes could help investigators find the criminals.

Juan Vucetich of the Argentine police also thought that fingerprints could be useful in criminal investigation. In 1891 he introduced a system for grouping prints into categories and comparing them. When some children were found murdered the following year, Vucetich analyzed bloody fingerprints at the scene. He showed that the prints matched the children's mother, and she was convicted of murder.

▶ FINGERPRINTS

Vucetich's work in Argentina helped make fingerprinting one of several forensic tools that became standard in the twentieth century. Police departments around the world took notice and began to apply the technique to their own cases. Fingerprinting is a good example of how forensic methods evolve over time as people invent new technologies and raise new questions.

Fingerprinting is possible because the skin at the tip of each human finger is covered by a dense pattern of narrow, raised ridges separated by valleys. Skin oil collects in the valleys. Whenever a person touches something, the oil is deposited in a pattern that matches the valleys. If the finger happens to be coated with blood or some other substance that can leave a mark, the prints will be highly visible. Most ordinary fingerprints are unseen, or latent, until a criminalist does something to make them visible.

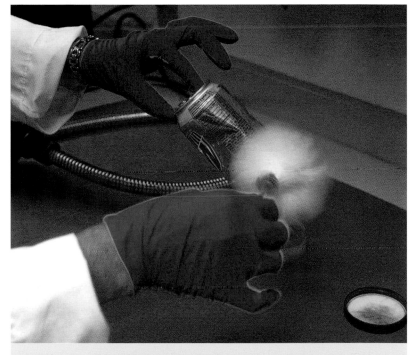

▲ Dusting a discarded beverage can with fine powder will reveal the latent, or hidden, fingerprints of the people who have handled the can.

Dusting, a traditional technique for making prints visible, is still used today. It involves swirling fine powder over places that might have fingerprints. The powder sticks to the oil of the latent prints, making them suddenly appear. Dusting is easiest to do on hard surfaces, such as windows or gun barrels. Prints on paper, fabric, and other soft surfaces may become visible, however, when sprayed with a chemical that reacts with skin oils. Forensic technicians can also make latent prints appear by using a chemical called cyanoacrylate, better known as superglue. When superglue is heated inside a closed container, it gives off a gas that fastens itself to traces of oil in the prints.

The most expensive and sensitive fingerprint recovery technique is called vacuum metal deposition (VMD). Developed in the 1970s, VMD has been used to recover prints from very soft and flexible surfaces, such as soft plastic supermarket bags. It may also work on pieces of evidence that have been submerged in water or exposed to weathering. VMD requires the evidence to be sealed in a special container. The air is pumped out of the container, creating a vacuum. Then metallic gases, usually zinc and gold, are pumped into the chamber. The metal vapors stick to the fingerprint oils, forming a thin film that reveals the shape of the prints in fine metallic lines.

Fingerprints are useless if criminalists can't compare them to something—to a known suspect, for example, or to a database of prints that have already been recorded. In the United States, that database is the Integrated Automated Fingerprint Identification System (IAFIS). In mid–2007 the IAFIS database contained the fingerprints of more than 47 million people. Most people represented in the database had

▲ An analyst compares a suspect's fingerprints (on the card) to prints in a database. Computers can match fingerprints, but such matches are verified by experienced fingerprint analysts.

been fingerprinted during arrest. Their prints were turned in to IAFIS by city, state, or federal law enforcement agencies.

A complete set of prints, or ten-print submission, contains a print from each finger. For years prints were obtained by inking the suspect's fingers and rolling them across white cards. Some prints are still collected that way, but many departments use digital scanners that read and copy fingerprints, sending them directly to IAFIS.

In addition to recording and storing fingerprints, the IAFIS software compares new prints to the database, looking for matches. Before fingerprint matching was computerized, it could take an expert analyst up to three months to search the files for a match to an unknown print. Now, however, fingerprint checks in criminal cases can be done in less than two hours, although experienced fingerprint analysts still carry out visual checks to confirm the matches that the computer makes. Fingerprint scanners have come into commercial use, too. Certain models of notebook computers have fingerprint-activated locks that only the owners can open.

What would crime shows—or real-life crime solving—be without fingerprints? Crime scenes do not always yield prints, but when prints do exist, they are usually seen as rock-solid evidence. Yet critics of finger-printing think that prints are being overused. Some people fear that the government wants to create a universal database that would allow all citizens to be identified and tracked by their fingerprints. Others simply question whether fingerprints really are unique identifiers. The fact that no duplicate fingerprints have ever been found does not mean that they never will be.

Finally, fingerprint analysis can be flawed. In 2004 FBI agents arrested and held Brandon Mayfield, an Oregon attorney, on the grounds that a fingerprint linked him to a recent terrorist bombing in Spain. Later, after admitting that it had bungled the finger-print analysis, the FBI released Mayfield and paid him damages for wrongful arrest.

▶ SCIENTIFIC SLEUTHS

Modern crime solving relies on a vast variety of forensic tools and techniques. Some of them are so complex that they require considerable special training. Take ballistics, the study of firearms and how they act. Ballistics is, in part, the science of tracing the path of bullets, which can help criminalists discover how a shooting happened. Another aspect of ballistics is firearms identification, which is finding out whether a bullet recovered from a crime scene or victim was fired from a particular gun.

▲ Measured in thousandths of an inch or in millimeters, the marks on this bullet may point to the person who fired the shot—if police find a gun that ballistics experts can use for a comparison shot.

To answer that question, the criminalist usually fires a new bullet from the gun in question. The firing occurs under controlled conditions, such as into a tub of water or gel that will keep the bullet from being damaged. The criminalist can then use a microscope to compare the two bullets, one from the crime and the other just fired. When a bullet passes through the barrel of the gun, the inside of the barrel creates marks called striations and crimps on the outer shell of the bullet. Firearms identification is based on the belief that every firearm produces a set of marks that are as unique as a fingerprint. This means that if the striations and crimps on two bullets match, they must have been fired by the same gun.

One of the most varied branches of forensics is trace evidence analysis. Trace evidence is any small amount of evidence left on a crime scene, victim, or criminal as a result of evidence exchange. A chip of fingernail polish, a few cat hairs, lint from the upholstery of a sofa, a human hair found on the victim that does not match the victim's hair—all are examples of trace evidence. So are tool marks, broken windows, footprints, and tire marks. Identifying a speck of nail polish may seem impossible, but skilled and experienced crime lab workers can determine the manufacturer, and sometimes the batch number, of the tiny sample. Sometimes the identification of a torn bus ticket or a tread mark from a bicycle tire turns an investigation in a new and successful direction. Arson investigation, which requires training in the physics of fire and the chemistry of accelerants, is another highly specialized branch of forensics.

The work of the crime scene technicians and criminalists who collect and examine evidence every day on the job is often supplemented by the knowledge and experience of experts in many fields. Most such forensic scientists are not full-time criminal investigators. They are teachers and researchers who apply their scientific specialties to criminal investigation. Some sciences that are especially useful in forensics are

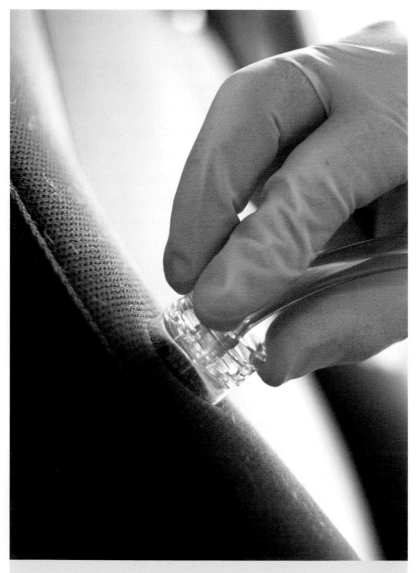

▲ Using a suction device, a technician gathers trace evidence from a car seat.

odontology, the study of teeth and bite marks; ento-
mology, the study of insects; and botany, the study of
plants (including pollen and seeds, which are often
part of the evidence at outdoor crime scenes).

Psychiatry has applications to forensics, too.
Psychiatrists examine suspects, for example, to determine whether they are mentally ill, or likely
to be lying. A related field is criminology, the study of
criminal minds and behavior. Criminologists often
contribute to investigations by reviewing the evidence
and then coming up with a profile for the criminal. In
the case of a serial murderer, for example, if a criminologist says that a criminal is likely to be a white
male in his thirties, investigators may narrow their
search for possible suspects by focusing on men who
match that description.

The range of forensic techniques is wide. Most
investigations do not need to draw on all of them.
Sometimes, however, tragedy or disaster on a massive
scale calls forth the forensic resources of an entire
region. In 2001, after the 9/11 terrorist attacks, forensic specialists in such fields as engineering, evidence
recovery, explosives, and human identification were
needed in New York City, Washington, D.C., and rural
Pennsylvania. Along with police, firefighters, and
other public servants, scores of criminalists and forensic
experts answered the call.

THE CHAIN OF CUSTODY

FROM THE START of each investigation, every piece of evidence must be carefully tracked to create a record called a chain of custody. The chain of custody tells where the evidence was at every moment, whether in a police car, a lab, an evidence locker, or a courtroom. The chain of custody also indicates who was responsible for the evidence at all times. Everyone who handles a piece of evidence must sign or initial it (or the evidence bag that contains it). Each signer adds the date and time he or she received the evidence.

The chain of custody reveals who collected the evidence, where it was kept, and who used it and why. An unbroken chain of custody means that each link in the chain—each person who handled the evidence—can state in a court of law that it is the same piece of evidence he or she received and passed on to the next link. Most crime labs and law enforcement departments that process large quantities of evidence now use computerized, password-protected laboratory information management systems (LIMS) to organize the many records in multiple chains of custody.

An unclear or broken chain can make it impossible to account for the evidence at every point in its journey. If the case comes to trial, the defendant's lawyers can suggest that the evidence may have been altered or faked. The defendant does not have to prove that this happened—raising doubt in the jurors' minds may be enough to bring a verdict of "not guilty." Evidence with a questionable chain of custody is often ruled inadmissible, which means that it cannot be used in court.

Like all physical evidence, paint samples from this car involved in a collision will be tracked through every step of the investigation, with paperwork to show who had the evidence at all times. If the records are incomplete or the samples are mishandled, the evidence may be worthless in court.

The 1995 murder trial of former football star O. J. Simpson is a notorious example of broken chains of custody. The prosecution—the state attorneys who charged Simpson with killing his former wife and one of her friends—seemed at first to have strong evidence. DNA tests showed that blood on several pieces of evidence came from Simpson and the two murdered people. During the trial, however, Simpson's attorneys hammered on gaps in the chains of custody. Some of the worst gaps concerned a sample of Simpson's blood and a bloody glove found at the scene. The defense attorneys argued that Simpson's blood could have been planted on the glove to incriminate him. In the end, the jury found Simpson not guilty. No one knows what the verdict would have been if the evidence had been properly handled.

A mystery in the scenic California mountain town of Mammoth Lakes drove investigators to use every possible forensic tool to identify an unknown victim.

203

Mammoth Lake

EXIT 1 MILE

CHAPTER FOUR

CASE FILE:
THE MYSTERY VICTIM OF MAMMOTH LAKES

▼ **OF ALL THE PUZZLES THAT DETECTIVES**

and crime scene investigators must try to solve, questions of identity are among the most challenging. When a case involves a mystery murder victim, or a suspect whose identity is unknown, criminalists use a variety of methods to discover the missing name.

Finding the name does not answer every question. Investigators must still determine what happened to the victim, and they must still track down the suspect. Yet discovering the identity of an unknown person is a key part of forensics. Even when other questions remain unanswered, knowing a victim's name may bring peace to family members who have searched for a missing person, perhaps for years.

Questions of identity lie at the heart of an ongoing case in Mammoth Lakes, a small mountain town on the eastern side of California's Sierra Nevada. In their search for answers, the investigators have used many forensic techniques. Some of their methods, such as interviewing witnesses, are traditional, tried-and-true tools. Others are on the cutting edge of forensic science, including techniques that had never before been used in a criminal investigation.

▶ A GRUESOME DISCOVERY

In May 2003 a man went hiking with his dog in the wooded slopes above the Shady Rest Campground in Mammoth Lakes. When the dog started sniffing something on the ground, the man took a look—and found himself staring at a human skull.

The hiker's find kicked off a quest for information. Law enforcement officers and scientists worked together to answer three questions: Whose skull was it? What had happened? If foul play was involved, who was guilty?

The first step was a search of the area where the skull had been found. A law enforcement officer discovered a shallow grave containing bones and pieces of dried, leathery human skin. Other body parts were scattered nearby. Coyotes and bears are numerous in the area, and it looked as if animals had opened the grave and disturbed the remains. Searchers also found

▲ A shoe was among the items of women's clothing found in or near the shallow grave of the Mammoth Lakes body.

some women's clothing and a wristwatch that was still running. None of the evidence recovered from the grave, however, gave a clue to the identity of the body.

▶ FIRST FORENSIC EXAMINATION

Mammoth Lakes is a small community. In twenty-five years, its police department had investigated just two murders. Like most police departments across the country, the Mammoth Lake department did not have its own forensic specialists or lab. The California Department of Justice sent a forensic team from the Fresno Regional

Case No. _____ FRO3-2753 _____ Date 7/1/04
Item No. _____ #21 _____ Analyst _____ SDL

▲ The unknown woman's wristwatch was still running when
law enforcement officials unearthed it, but it bore no name
or other clue to its wearer's identity.

Crime Lab to process the crime scene, although
Detective Paul Dostie of the Mammoth Lakes Police
Department (MLPD) remained in charge of the case.

The forensic team collected the victim's remains
and sent them to the office of the medical examiner in
San Francisco. The examiner reported that the body
was that of a woman between thirty and forty years
old. She had been between 54 and 57 inches tall (4.5
feet, or a little more). She might have been Asian.
Finally, the unknown victim had been dead between

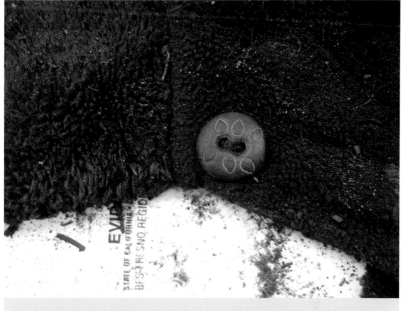

▲ A coat with a distinctive button is another piece of recovered evidence that may someday help link the Mammoth Lakes victim to her killer.

six and nine months. She had spent the winter of 2002–2003 in her mountain grave.

▶ **THE WITNESSES' STORY**

Dostie focused on the possibility that the mystery woman was Asian, because that suggestion fit in with another lead he had received. Several weeks after the discovery of the remains, employees of the Mammoth Lakes U.S. Forest Service Visitor Center contacted the MLPD. The employees had remembered that months earlier, in the fall of 2002, a man and a woman had stopped at the Visitor Center to ask about campsites. The man had seemed rude and mean. The woman— who was short and looked Asian—had confided to one of the employees that he was her husband and that she was afraid of him.

Dostie called in a forensic artist from the Los Angeles County Sheriff's Department. Working with the Forest Service employees, the artist drew sketches that represented the visitors as the employees remembered them. Dostie circulated the sketches throughout the region, but no one recognized either the man or the woman. The remains found in the shallow grave did not fit the description of anyone who had been reported missing.

Today most people know that one of the most accurate forms of identification is DNA, the unique genetic fingerprint that each individual carries in the cells of blood, saliva, and body tissues. Yet DNA from a victim or a suspect is useless unless there is something to compare it with. In the case of a crime suspect, the suspect's DNA must match DNA that was found on the victim or at the scene of the crime. In the case of an unknown person like the Mammoth Lakes mystery woman, the best chance of making an identification is to match DNA from the body to one of the more than 4 million samples that are recorded in the Combined DNA Index System (CODIS), the nation's law enforcement database of genetic profiles. DNA was available from the woman's remains, but there was no match at CODIS. With no samples for comparison, the possibility of genetic identification seemed closed. For a year Detective Dostie explored several theories—one idea was that the woman was an Asian mail-order bride—but he found no answers.

▶ DIGGING DEEPER INTO DNA

The Mammoth Lakes case took a new direction in 2004, when Dostie heard from another law enforcement officer about a Florida company that was using DNA to identify a person's ethnic background according to the proportions of European, East Asian, African, and Native American ancestry represented in a DNA sample. The technique, called DNAWitness 2.5, was not yet available in government-run crime labs, but Dostie sent a piece of the woman's thighbone to Florida. Marrow inside the bone contained DNA, which, according to the test, showed that the woman was 100 percent American Indian.

Was the woman Asian, as the San Francisco medical examiner and the Forest Service witnesses had thought, or was she American Indian, as the Florida DNA test said? Dostie decided to ask a physical anthropologist, a scientist who studies and compares human physical features. A call to the American

Association of Physical Anthropologists put him in touch with Phillip Walker, who was president of the association at the time. Walker, an authority on California's prehistoric American Indians, agreed to look at the Mammoth Lakes mystery remains.

Walker's examination led him to several conclusions. First, based on the woman's size, hair color, and skull shape, he was convinced that she was American Indian, probably from Mesoamerica, the region that includes Mexico and northern Central America. Second, he located several narrow, sharp-edged slits in what remained of the skin of her abdomen—slits that did not look like animal bites.

From the start, Detective Dostie had been certain that the mystery woman was a murder victim. People found in hidden, illegal graves, he pointed out, usually get there through foul play. Now he knew that she was probably stabbed to death.

Walker thought of a way to check his idea that the woman was an American Indian from Mesoamerica. At the anthropologist's suggestion, Dostie sent a sample of the victim's DNA to a California research lab, where it was analyzed for material called human leukocyte antigen (HLA) genes. The analysis showed two closely related forms of HLA on a single chromosome, or strand of genetic material. This condition is rare in the total human population, but common among American Indians. The researcher who analyzed the HLA agreed with Walker that the victim was probably Mexican or Central American.

▶ YOU ARE WHAT YOU EAT

With the focus shifted to Mesoamerica, Walker started thinking about Oaxaca, a state in western Mexico. Many of the Mexicans who have immigrated to central California are from Oaxaca. Was the mystery woman of Mammoth Lakes one of them? Maybe isotopes could answer that question.

Isotopes are slightly different forms of atoms of the same chemical element. Scientists have learned that certain foods contain specific combinations of carbon and nitrogen isotopes. The isotopes found in water also vary from place to place. People's bodies are made up of the atoms that they consumed as food and drink. By analyzing the isotopes in tissue samples, a scientist can determine that the people who provided the samples have eaten certain kinds of food or have come from certain places.

Walker sent samples from the mystery woman to a geochemist named Henry Schwarcz at McMaster University in Ontario, Canada. During his career Schwarcz had examined samples from mummies thousands of years old, shedding light on what ancient people ate, but he had never used the technique on a modern crime victim. After analyzing the mystery woman's hair, teeth, and bones, Schwarcz decided that she had eaten a diet high in corn and had drunk water from western Mexico—specifically, from Oaxaca.

▶ MATCHING MITOCHONDRIAL DNA

Dostie's next step involved the mystery woman's mitochondrial DNA, or mtDNA. This part of the genetic code is passed from mother to daughter. Genetic researchers use it to trace people's maternal ancestry. To study the connections and migrations of ancient people in the Americas, the University of California at Davis has built a database of more than three thousand mtDNA samples from many modern American Indian groups. Walker and Dostie sent the mystery woman's DNA to Davis to be tested against the database. Amazingly, there was a match—to a woman who lived in the village of San Mateo Macuilxochitl in Oaxaca. The match meant that the mystery victim and the San Mateo woman shared a female ancestor, possibly as distant as a great-great-great-grandmother.

Unfortunately, the woman in San Mateo said that she did not know anything about the mystery victim. This was not necessarily surprising—the number of women descended from the same great-great-great-grandmother could be very large. But with the link to Oaxaca established, Dostie found another resource. Ray Morales, president of a Oaxacan business association in Los Angeles, travels frequently to Oaxaca. He agreed to circulate pictures of the mystery victim there. By this time, the sketch created by the forensic artist was not the only image of the mystery woman. Dostie now had a three-dimensional model. Betty Pat Gatliff, a forensic artist from Oklahoma who is known for sculpting clay reconstructions of unknown dead persons, had created a life-sized likeness of the mystery victim's face.

▶ FACIAL RECONSTRUCTION

Facial reconstruction is both an art and a science. Reconstructors usually begin with a plaster, wax, or plastic mold of the skull—or as many pieces of the skull as are available. Then they build up a picture of what the face over that skull might have looked like. Some reconstructive artists draw or paint, and some use computer programs to create digital images. Others, like Gatliff, work with clay.

Reconstructive artists use a variety of techniques, along with experience, intuition, and artistic judgment, to give faces to the dead. Some base their approach on

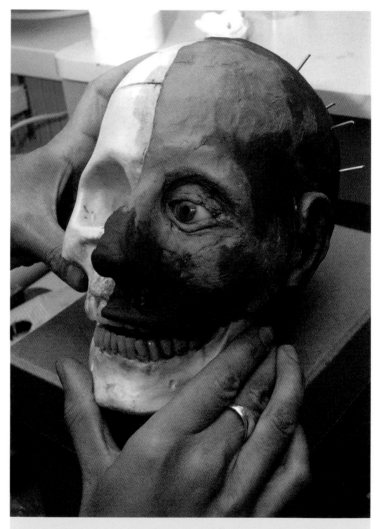

▲ Combining scientific data with experience and intuition, a facial reconstruction artist builds a model that may spark a memory—and possibly an identification—in witnesses.

anatomy, the study of the body's structure. They start with the shape of the skull and build up a face one muscle at a time. Others rely on **morphometry**, or measurements of the average thickness of the flesh over many points on the typical human face. Most use a combination of techniques to recapture the way flesh and skin sit atop bone.

The more a reconstructive artist knows about the unidentified person, the better. If forensic specialists have offered reasonable ideas about the person's gender, age, race, or overall health, these factors influence the morphometric data that the artist uses. Any remaining soft tissues—ears, eyes and eyelids, or lips—will help the artist match the dead person's appearance. In the case of the Mammoth Lakes victim, however, the only useful remains other than the skull were bits of the woman's dark hair.

Gatliff finished her clay model of the unknown woman's head with skin-colored paint, a dark wig, and brown eyes. When Detective Dostie saw the model, he was startled by how closely it resembled the artist's drawing of the woman who had stopped at the Forest Service Visitor Center. Because Gatliff had never seen the drawing, Dostie was more sure than ever that the victim found in the shallow grave was the same woman who had confided her fear to employees at the

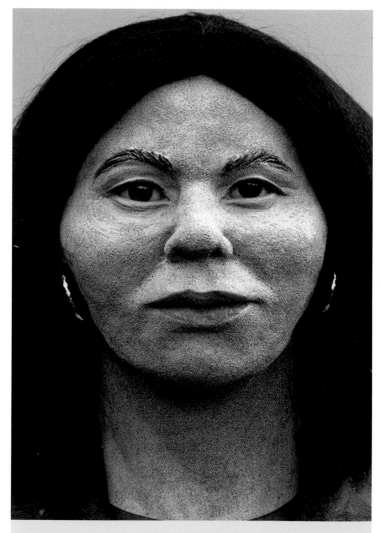

▲ This facial reconstruction of the Mammoth Lakes victim led police to a name: Barbara. They are still hoping to confirm her identity, and to discover how she met her death.

Visitor Center. The two images were as close to a portrait of the dead woman as the detective could possibly get. Now all he could do was wait and see if someone, anyone, recognized her.

▶ ANSWERS AND QUESTIONS

One of Ray Morales's trips to Mexico brought a breakthrough. A woman in Oaxaca identified the woman in the pictures as her stepdaughter, Barbara, whom she had not seen for seven years. According to the stepmother, Barbara's biological parents were both long dead. Barbara had a sister and two sons, but their whereabouts were unknown.

The best way to know for certain whether the Mammoth Lakes victim is Barbara would be to compare her DNA to that of a parent, sibling, or child. Morales got a DNA sample from one of Barbara's nieces, but it did not permit a firm identification. In mid–2007 Dostie and others were working to find more of Barbara's relatives, especially her sons. If they can locate and test one of her children, they will know for sure whether Barbara was the body found at Mammoth Lakes.

Meanwhile, Walker has suggested another test called tooth cementum annulation (TCA). This technique counts the layers of cementum, or hardened tissue, around the roots of teeth, with each layer representing a year. In forensics, TCA is usually used to estimate how old a person was when he or she died, but some researchers think that cementum layers may hold additional information. Physical stresses such as pregnancy and childbirth may be encoded in the layers. If this is true, and the Mammoth Lakes victim's TCA turns out to match the known childbearing history of Barbara from Oaxaca, the teeth will be another piece of evidence for identification.

A lot of evidence points toward the identification, but none of the evidence proves beyond doubt that the victim *is* Barbara. Still, Detective Paul Dostie is fairly certain of it. He also thinks that the man who came to the Visitor Center with Barbara in the fall of 2002 was her husband—and probably her murderer. Some day, Dostie believes, someone who sees the sketches or descriptions of the couple will call in a tip that will help police identify Barbara's husband—and track him down.

"When we get that tip," Dostie wrote in *Forensic Magazine* in 2007, "that'll be huge. Her DNA could still be somewhere in the suspect's car, house, or apartment—on a hairbrush or old toothbrush. That would end the case right there, if we could put her DNA on him. The first question I want to ask him: Why didn't you report your wife missing?"

► WHAT DOES FORENSIC SCIENCE DO?

The Mammoth Lakes mystery shows that even with the most advanced scientific tools and techniques, including some that are new to criminal investigation, it can be extremely hard to identify an unknown victim or suspect with 100 percent certainty. But the Mammoth Lakes case also shows how much a determined and well-trained investigator can learn from the evidence of a crime.

One of the pioneers of forensics in twentieth-century America was Paul Kirk, who worked in one of the nation's first crime labs and helped start one of its first programs of forensic studies, at the University of California. Kirk also wrote an early forensics textbook called *Crime Investigation.* In this book, published in 1953, Kirk said, "Wherever [the criminal] steps, whatever he touches, whatever he leaves, even unconsciously, will serve as silent witness against him. Not only his fingerprints or his footprints, but his hair, the fibers from his clothing, the glass he breaks, the tool mark he leaves, the paint he scratches. . . . All of these and more bear mute witness against him. This is evidence that does not forget."

Kirk was right. Evidence does not forget—but it needs someone to give it a voice so that it can tell its story. The duty of the criminalist and the forensic scientist is to give the evidence that voice.

THE TWO WESTS

THE CHANCE OF ANY two people having identical sets of body measurements was about one in 286 million, claimed French criminologist and police officer Alphonse Bertillon. He was the inventor of *bertillonage*, a method of using measurements—such as the length of the ears, the size of the head, and the width of the shoulders—to tell one person from another and identify individuals. In 1903, twenty years after Bertillon introduced his system, a case at the Leavenworth Penitentiary in Kansas showed that even unlikely events sometimes happen.

When a prisoner named Will West was sent to the penitentiary, the clerk assigned to take West's *bertillonage* measurements thought that the new convict looked familiar, but West said he had never been in the prison before. The clerk checked the prison's *bertillonage* records and discovered that another man with the same body measurements was already serving time in Leavenworth—under the name William West!

Prison officials placed the two Wests in the same room and could hardly tell them apart. The only reliable way prison officials could tell William from Will was through their fingerprints. The case revealed the weaknesses in Bertillon's identification system, which was soon abandoned in favor of fingerprinting.

As for the two Wests, their resemblance was probably more than a remarkable coincidence. Although they claimed not to know each other, rumors at the time said that they were related. In the 1980s researchers found evidence suggesting that the Wests may have been brothers, perhaps even identical twins.

A New York City police officer takes a bertillonage measurement. This photograph dates from around 1908, when the French system of body measurement was still used as identification. Soon it would be dropped in favor of fingerprinting.

▼ GLOSSARY

accelerant a substance that can be used to start, spread, or increase the destructive power of fires

autopsy a medical examination performed on a body to find the cause of death; a forensic autopsy also tries to establish the time and manner of death

ballistics the branch of forensic science that deals with guns, gunshot patterns, and bullets

chain of custody written record of the history of each piece of evidence from crime scene to trial, with information about everyone who has handled the evidence and why

criminalistics the part of forensic science that deals with gathering and examining evidence from crime scenes

criminology the study of criminals and their behavior

DNA deoxyribonucleic acid, the substance that contains each individual's genetic code and is found in blood, saliva, and other tissues from the body

DNA testing the use of DNA to identify individuals; DNA testing may match a person to a piece of evidence or establish a blood relationship between two people

evidence exchange principle the idea that whenever two objects (or people) contact each other, they exchange material; sometimes called Locard's exchange principle

facial reconstruction creation of a drawing, clay model, or computer image of the head of an unidentified person based on the skull or skull fragments

forensic science the use of scientific knowledge or methods to investigate crimes, identify suspects, and try criminal cases in court

forensics in general, debate or review of any question of fact relating to the law; often used to refer to the solving of crimes by means of science

homicide murder

medical examiner (ME) public official responsible for determining cause of death (sometimes called coroner)

morphometry measurement of the depth of flesh over bone; used in facial reconstruction

postmortem after death; postmortem injuries to a body, for example, occurred after the person died

serology the branch of medical and forensic science that deals with blood

taphonomy the study of the physical changes in a body after death

toxicology the branch of medical, environmental, and forensic science that deals with drugs, poisons, and harmful substances

trace evidence very small amounts of evidence, such as carpet fiber, hair, or paint chips, left at a crime scene or on a suspect by the evidence exchange principle

▼ FIND OUT MORE

FURTHER READING

Campbell, Andrea. *Forensic Science: Evidence, Clues, and Investigation.* Philadelphia: Chelsea House, 2000.

Fridell, Ron. *DNA Fingerprinting: The Ultimate Identity.* New York: Franklin Watts/Scholastic, 2001.

Friedlander, Mark Jr., and Terry Phillips. *When Objects Talk: Solving a Crime with Science.* Minneapolis, MN: Lerner, 2001.

Funkhluser, John. *Forensic Science for High School Students.* Dubuque, IA: Kendall Hunt, 2005.

Jackson, Donna. *The Wildlife Detectives: How Forensic Scientists Fight Crimes Against Nature.* Boston: Houghton Mifflin, 2000.

Mattern, Joanne. *Forensics.* San Diego, CA: Blackbirch, 2004.

Owen, David. *Police Lab: How Forensic Science Tracks Down and Convicts Criminals.* Toronto: Firefly, 2002.

Platt, Richard. *Crime Scene: The Ultimate Guide to Forensic Science.* New York: Dorling Kindersley, 2003.

Yeatts, Tabatha. *Forensics: Solving the Crime.* Minneapolis, MN: Oliver, 2001.

WEB SITES

www.aafs.org/yfsf/index.htm

The Web site of the American Academy of Forensic Sciences features the Young Forensic Scientists Forum, with information on careers in forensics. The site also links to other Internet resources.

www.courttv.com/forensics_curriculum/
Developed by CourtTV (now TruTV), the American Academy of Forensic Sciences, and the National Science Teachers Association, this kid-friendly Forensics in the Classroom site introduces forensic science with a glossary, time line, and virtual forensics lab.

www.crimezzz.net/forensic_history/index.htm
The Crimeline page offers a brief time line of developments in forensic science from prehistory to the present.

www.fbi.gov/hq/lab/handbook/intro.htm
The FBI's online *Handbook of Forensic Sciences* gives detailed instructions on how to collect, preserve, and examine evidence.

www.forensicmag.com/
Forensic Magazine's Web page features case studies and news about developments in criminalistics and other branches of forensic science.

www.sciencenewsforkids.org/articles/20041215/Feature1.asp
Science News for Kids features this article on crime labs and what they do, with links to additional sites and a brief history of forensic science.

▼ BIBLIOGRAPHY

The author found these books and articles especially helpful when researching this volume.

Bell, Suzanne. *Encyclopedia of Forensic Science.* New York: Facts On File, 2004.

Bisbing, Richard E. "Locard Exchange: Fractured Patterns: Microscopical Examination of Real Physical Evidence," *Modern Microscopy Journal,* January 29, 2004, http://www.modernmicroscopy.com/main.asp?article=11&print=true

Chisum, W. Jerry, and Brent E. Turvey. "Evidence Dynamics: Locard's Exchange Principle and Crime Reconstruction," *Journal of Behavioral Profiling,* January 2000, 1(1), http://www.profiling.org/journal/vol1_no1/jbp_ed_january2000_1-1.html

Dostie, Paul. "Case Number 03-0929: Murder in Mammoth Lakes," *Forensic Magazine,* June/July 2007, http://www.forensicmag.com/articles.asp?pid=150

Fisher, Barry, David Fisher, and Jason Kolowski. *Forensics Demystified.* New York: McGraw-Hill, 2006.

Genge, Ngaire E. *The Forensic Casebook: The Science of Crime Scene Investigation.* New York: Ballantine, 2002.

Gillespie, Helen. "Computers and the Science of Solving Crime," *Today's Chemist at Work,* November 1997, 6(9), pp. 40–44, http://pubs.acs.org/hotartcl/tcaw/97/nov/hancock.html

James, Stuart H., and Jon J. Nordby, eds. *Forensic Science: An Introduction to Scientific and Investigative Techniques,* 2nd ed. London: CRC Press, 2005.

Lovgren, Stefan. "'CSI Effect' Is Mixed Blessing for Real Crime Labs," *National Geographic News,* September 23, 2004, http://news.nationalgeographic.com/news/2004/09/0923_040923_csi.htm

Page, Douglas. "Four Years to Day One: A Saga of Science and Inquest," *Forensic Magazine,* June/July 2007, www.forensicmag.com/articles.asp?pid=151

Ramsland, Katherine. *The C.S.I. Effect.* New York: Berkley, 2006.

Sachs, Jessica Snyder. *Corpse: Nature, Forensics, and the Struggle to Pinpoint Time of Death.* Cambridge, MA: Perseus, 2001.

Saferstein, Richard. *Criminalistics: An Introduction to Forensic Science.* Upper Saddle River, NJ: Prentice Hall, 2003.

Toobin, Jeffrey. "The CSI Effect: The Truth About Forensic Science," *The New Yorker,* May 7, 2007, pp. 30–35.

Trimm, Harold H. *Forensics the Easy Way.* Hauppage, NY: Barron's, 2005.

Wecht, Cyril, and Greg Saitz. *Mortal Evidence: The Forensics Behind Nine Shocking Cases.* Amherst, NY: Prometheus, 2003.

▼ INDEX

Page numbers in **boldface** are illustrations.

REBECCA STEFOFF has written many books on scientific subjects for young readers. She has explored the world of evolutionary biology in Marshall Cavendish's Family Trees series; she also wrote *Microscopes and Telescopes* and *The Camera* for the same publisher's Great Inventions series. After publishing *Charles Darwin and the Evolution Revolution* (Oxford University Press, 1996), Stefoff appeared in the *A&E Biography* program on Darwin and his work. She lives in Portland, Oregon. You can learn more about her books for young readers at **www.rebeccastefoff.com**.